LIFE AS REVEALED BY THE HOLY SPIRIT

Dr TEMI .O. UWEN

Copyright © 2005 by Dr. Temi O. Uwen

Life As Revealed By The Holy Spirit
by Dr. Temi O. Uwen

Printed in the United States of America

ISBN 1-59781-717-1

All rights reserved solely by the author. The author guarantees all contents are original and do not infringe upon the legal rights of any other person or work. No part of this book may be reproduced in any form without the permission of the author. The views expressed in this book are not necessarily those of the publisher.

Unless otherwise indicated, Bible quotations are taken from:
    King James Bible and the AMPLIFIED BIBLE, Copyright © 1987 by Zondervan.

www.xulonpress.com

I give God thanks for these revelations He gave me through the Holy Spirit which I decided to put into writing. I thank God for His grace to be able to share these messages with you. I have prayed for you who will read this book, I know the eyes of your understanding will be enlightened and you will experience victory and breakthrough in every aspect of your life. Remember that we all with open face beholding as in a glass the glory of the Lord, are changed into the same image from glory to glory, even as by the Spirit of the Lord.

God bless you as you read.

CONTENTS

DEDICATION xi

ACKNOWLEDGEMENT xiii

ENDORSEMENT xv

FOREWORD xvii

CHAPTER

1. SITUATIONS AND CIRCUMSTANCES   PART 1 21

2. SITUATIONS AND CIRCUMSTANCES   PART 2 27

3. THE WORD OF GOD   PART 1 33

4. UNBELIEF 35

5. MONEY 39

6. PRAYER 45

7. MEDITATION 49

8. TRUSTING GOD..53

9. THE WORD OF GOD   PART 2 59

10. THE INVISIBLE THAT BECOMES THE VISIBLE 63

11. DIVORCE (" THORN IN THE FLESH ") 67

BIOGRAPHY

Dr Uwen is a practicing medical doctor who has practiced medicine in the West Indies as well as the United Kingdom. She is currently majoring in the field of psychiatry.

She has been a Christian for a long time and have learned from many great teachers of the word of God. She is a member of a local church. She had her christian foundation in Africa.

DEDICATION

This book is dedicated to God Almighty; the one that was, and is, and is to come

To Him that sits upon the throne and unto the Lamb, be the Glory forever

To my father, the Lord almighty whose dominion endureth for ever

Father, I am eternally grateful to you

Thank you for endorsing me with your Spirit that enabled me to write this book and continuously revealing to me by your Spirit the understanding of life.

TO YOU BE THE GLORY AND HONOR AND POWER FOREVER AND EVER, AMEN.

ACKNOWLEDGEMENT

I will like to acknowledge the following people for their contribution and support to writing of this book and others for their contribution to my life one way or the other.

First of all, I will like to acknowledge my precious husband, John Uwen for his love, understanding and support during the period of writing this book. God bless you dear. Also our children, Jessica, John(Jnr) and Jemima. God abundantly bless all of you. You are great children and mummy loves you all.

I will like to acknowledge my parents, my late father, Dr D.A.Ogbe for his contribution to my life and also my mother, Alice who is relentless in praying for me and my siblings. God bless you, mum; you are an inspiration.

I will also like to acknowledge my siblings; Rowland, Patience, Stanley, Sonia and Lina for their encouragement. God bless all of you. Sonia, thanks for the time you gave proofreading and editing this book.

I will also like to acknowledge Mr & Mrs W. Iyonsi and their children, Bami and Bright for the role they play in my life. Bami you are a sister indeed. God bless all of you.

I will like to acknowledge Bishop D. Ibeleme for his labour of love, his support and immense contribution to making my dream a reality. May God richly reward you for all you did.

I will also like to acknowledge Bishop A. Njeri for her support and her friendship. You are greatly appreciated. God bless you.

Finally, I will like to acknowledge Pastors Vivian and Samuel Akinbaro for their support and prayers rendered for this book. God richly bless you both.

ENDORSEMENTS

Many believers today are struggling with the whole concept of hearing from God. Others on the other hand are uncomfortable with the idea of getting a word from God for the larger body of Christ. I want to thank Sister Temi Uwen for being sensitive to the word of God primarily for herself and secondarily for being generous and kind enough to share with the Church that which the Lord has revealed to her in the privacy of her fellowship with Him.

This book is broad based, covering a wide range of issues that affect our relationship with God and other believers. It will be a very helpful tool in our private devotions and I am convinced that many deep seated questions in the hearts of a lot of believers will be answered through it.

I am particularly impressed with the chapters on money, prayer and divorce. I thank Sister Temi for sharing the things that I believe will help to solidify a lot of marriages, heal family hurts and prevent divorce. I highly recommend this simple but powerful book.

Bishop (Dr) David Ibeleme
Victorious Faith Ministries, Trinidad & Tobago

Temi has done a good job of outlining the crucial issues which we all face in our everyday lives. Life as revealed by the Holy Spirit contains keys to living life in victory, life as God intended it.

Vivian Akinbaro, Co-Pastor
Eagles Assembly Church, London UK

Life as revealed by the Holy Spirit is a true revelation epistle. Considering circumstances and situations in life, you will only be able to go through them as per the revelation of the Holy Spirit.

Unbelief is a strong weapon that the enemy uses to fight against the revelation of whom God's word says you are. You need spiritual wisdom which is a practical thing to give to you understanding concerning money. As you meditate God's word, you will see the invisible things becoming visible realities transfering your thoughts from the zone of limitations to the zone of no limitations. This is what Temi has called Life as revealed by the Holy Spirit. I encourage you to read on guaranting you will not be disappointed. Every chapter of this book is a true revelation.

Bishop Annie Njeri
Brooks of Life Ministries, Airport Church, London UK

Foreword

At every point in time in our lives, there is always something happening good or bad within the sphere of our lives. These are called situations and circumstances.

Some people describe life as being up and down. Your life is not up and down because **it is hid with Christ in God (Colossians 3v3)**. It is that situation or circumstance that is up and down, not your life. The bible says in **Proverbs 4v18 that the path of the just is as a shining light, that shineth more and more unto the perfect day.** This means bad situation or circumstance happening around you, does not mean your life is getting worse but better. The bible says in **Ephesians 2v10 that we are His workmanship, created in Christ Jesus unto good works, which God hath before ordained that we should walk in them.** Your destiny does not change despite your situation or circumstance. What God has for you, His thoughts, plans and purposes for you which He had preordained (before the foundation of the world) that you should walk therein cannot be changed by bad situation or circumstance. For example, Saul the persecutor of christians became Paul a saint of God. Abram(childless) became

Abraham(father of many nations). Take a look at Joseph, the bad situation of being in prison, did not mean his life was getting worse or hath got worse.

Differentiate your life from your situation or circumstance. Situation and circumstance is not your life, rather these are external forces. You are a born again child of God, recreated after the image and the likeness of God. You have coded in you God's DNA and you carry God in you **with whom is no variableness neither shadow of turning (James 1v17b)**. You therefore have maximum stability in your life. **I am confident of this very thing, that He which hath begun a good work in you will perform it until the day of Jesus Christ (Philippians 1v6)**. Satan cannot stop that work, amen. Joseph despite the bad situation (being in prison) did not stop him from becoming a prime minister even in a foreign land, Egypt. This is because his life hidden with Christ is separate from his situation or circumstance. Our path surely shineth more and more unto the perfect day.

The word of God supersedes and overshadows every situation or circumstance. To the user it is a weapon of offence or defence, being the **the sword of the Spirit (Ephesians 6v17)**. The bible describes it **as spirit and as life. You are an offspring of that word (the incorruptible word of God), 1 Peter 1v23**. Your life therefore cannot be shaken in Christ Jesus; **Christ is your life (Colossians 3v4a)**. Christ said in **John 16v33 that He has told us these things, so that in Him we may have [perfect] peace and confidence. In the world you have tribulation and trials and distress and frustration; but be of good cheer [take courage; be confident, certain, undaunted]! For I have**

overcome the world. [I have deprived it of power to harm you and have conquered it for you.]

The bible says **ye are gods, and all of you are children of the most High, (Psalms 82v6)**. You are therefore in charge. Think on this.

Life as revealed by the Holy Spirit reveals the secrets of life; it's principles, operations and ways of tackling it using the word of God. This book is like a seed, it is fully packaged. Read it, study it and meditate on it and you will profit from it maximally.

God bless you.

How do you maintain your stability and receive a reward despite your situations and circumstances? Find out for yourself as you read.

Every situation and circumstance will demand a reaction but we must only provide a response. A reaction is governed by the situation and circumstance. A response is governed by the heart condition of the man facing the circumstance.

1.

CIRCUMSTANCES AND SITUATIONS PART 1

In every sphere of our lives we face different situations and circumstances. In this book, I will be discussing how wrong or bad situation and circumstance can influence our expectations and decisions. We will also be looking at how to remain firm despite all odds that stand against us getting our desired result.

Expectations

My expectations must be based on the word of God, as revealed by the Holy Spirit and not on my situations and circumstances. According to Him, when I base my expectation on my situation and circumstance, it means I am trusting in unstable things because they are subject to change.

Satan uses situation and circumstance to try to influence our expectation. He wants us to give up before the manifestation of the things we desire. When we yield to these situation and circumstance we become double minded. The Spirit of truth reminded me of the double minded man in **James 1v8**. This man is unstable in all his ways and therefore cannot receive anything from God. But the unwavering man, his expectation will be met. His expectation will not be cut off according to **Proverbs 23v18:** *For surely there is an end; and thine expectation shall not be cut off.* **Let us make sure our expectations are from the Lord.**

Decisions

Learn not to react to situations and circumstances, the Holy Spirit continued his ministration to me. Do not let them influence your mind negatively because they change and are unstable. You will make wrong decisions if they are based on situations and circumstances.

Do not let situation and circumstance dictate to you whether you made the right decision or not. The word of God should be your guide which dictates this to you, making you aware whether you have made a right or wrong decision. **Decisions should be made based on the word of God.** Decision is a stable element while situation and circumstance are unstable elements. Indecision is equally an unstable element. Why do you then wait for unstable elements to dictate to you what to do.

Also give no place to neutrality. Indecision and neutrality are open doors for the devil to come in to manipulate you. How? Through situation and circumstance. A man of decision is a man in charge of his destiny. You do not have a grip with your circumstance and situation but you have a grip on your decisions. Until you decide (that is have a grip), you are indirectly or directly influenced by situations and circumstances, unfortunately.

Take the man of integrity; He is one who keeps his word despite situation and circumstance, he does not let these dictate to him what to do. The man of integrity is a stable man (not double minded), his yea is yea and nay is nay. He operates from his heart (the inner man), not his mind or soulish realm. He is in control or in charge of his environment. He is not a man pleaser but God pleaser.

Every dream, every goal starts from a decision. A decision made from a reasonable time out in thinking will stand and will not be easily shaken. It cannot be tossed to and fro. Remember the man that built his house on the rock; when rain, flood and winds came at it, the house could not be brought down (**Matthew 7v24-25:** *THEREFORE whosoever heareth these sayings of mine, and doeth them, I will liken him unto a wise man, which built his house upon a rock: And the rain descended, and the floods came, and the winds blew, and beat upon that house; and it fell not: for it* *was founded upon a rock*). Decisions that are unshakable are from the heart.

Decisions and Commitments

Commitment starts from a decision. No decision, no commitment. Decision is a point of reference you can always look back to. Decision is taking control of your future in your today. Decision brings about discipline (self control). Self control means putting yourself under in order to conform to your decision made. How do you recognise a man of decision or a decisive man, it is by his discipline (self control).

Decision is a firm acclamation of the choice you are making.

Consequences of Bad Decisions

The concept of blame arise mostly when decisions are based on situation and circumstance. When these do not eventually favour us, we tend to blame ourselves. If a decision is from your heart, stay firm regardless of the situation and circumstance and your decision will eventually be.

It is difficult to locate or pinpoint where an actual problem really is if your decisions are based on situations and circumstances and things do not go the way you want. But if your decision is from the heart then you are able to locate the actual problem and know why things did not go the way you wanted.

Faith starts from when you make up your mind about something, that is making a decision. Example, even our salvation started from a decision made that we wanted to accept Jesus Christ as our Lord and saviour.

It is the carnal christian that reacts to situation and circumstance and hence will not get a blessing.

Reacting to words spoken by others is also reacting to situations and circumstances.

Distraction is another consequence of poor decision. A distracted person is one who reacts to situations and circumstances. He never achieves his goals or visions or dreams as a result of this. He is an easy prey for the devil since the devil operates through situations and circumstances to disuade him. A distracted person is a double minded man. You have to make things around you to conform to your dreams, visions and plans. How? By putting things in place, for example a plan, a timetable, or anything that can channel you or direct you or propel you to that decision made or goal or dream.

Impulsive decisions are not from the heart but are made based on situation and circumstance, hence they are difficult to keep because they have no substance. Remember the man that built his house on sandy soil; the rain, flood and winds were able to pull it down. (***Matthew 7v26-27:*** *And every one that heareth these sayings of mine, and doeth them not, shall be likened unto a foolish man, which built his house upon the sand: and the rain descended, and the floods came, and the winds blew, and beat upon that house; and it fell: and great was the fall of it.* So are impulsive decisions, they can easily be destroyed.

LEARN TO SAY NO TO SITUATIONS AND CIRCUMSTANCES.

Look for the root of a problem, attack and destroy it and

you will have rest. If you respond to what it's fruits are which are situations and circumstances, you will not have rest, it will still be raising up it's head, it is never solved.

To keep Satan defeated, you will have to continually operate from your inner man. You must learn not to react to situations and circumstances because that is how the devil can steal from you, try to destroy or kill you. A spiritually minded man only responds to his inner man, not situations and circumstances, hence he gets a blessing.

Perfect example is Jesus Christ, He never reacted to situations and circumstances, hence he could tell God to forgive those that crucified him. He also knew the real truth behind his death (that is the root of the matter).

Depression comes from giving over yourself either directly or indirectly, completely to a situation or circumstance. This now control you and hence dictates to you how you live. This is the same principle with addiction or a bad habit like overeating etc. You are no longer in charge, you have lost your self control and you are suppose to have the spirit of self control. When the devil gets you to a point that you have lost self control in one area of your life, he then comes in to manipulate your life. Why? In order to destroy you.

The reverse is the case when you give your life completely and totally to God and His Word, His Spirit now takes control of you. In this case the Holy Spirit does not manipulate you but guides you in order to manifest in you life and life in abundance. (**John 10v10b:** *I am come that they might have life, and that they might have it more abundantly.*)

Do you know you never loose no matter your situation and circumstance, you win all the time. Find out why.

2.

SITUATIONS AND CIRCUMSTANCES PART 2

The devil operates by using situations and circumstances. These are unstable elements and are always changing. No matter the situation and circumstance the devil presents, always remember it is not exactly what he portrays it to be. It may look like you cannot make it, it may look like you have failed, do not be discouraged stay with God's evidence (His word). At the end of the day the truth always outlives a lie. The truth is what you believe God for or prayed about will surely come to pass.

Know it, **the devil's nature is to fail**, so he fails in everything he does. So remember that a situation or circumstance portraying as if he (the devil) has won, is not really the case because he cannot win, he loses all the time. So watch that situation or circumstance blow up in his face as usual. Remember, no matter how it seems, the devil will surely lose because he is already a loser and can never win, no matter if he tries to win because loosing is his nature.

God is a winner, He wins all the time. Following Jesus death, it looked like satan had succeeded and Jesus Christ had failed. The situation looked like that was the case, but it was not the truth. The resurrection of Jesus Christ proved what the actual truth had been from the beginning. See **1 Corinthians 2v6-8:** *HOWBEIT we speak wisdom among them that are perfect: yet not the wisdom of this world, nor of the princes of this world, that come to nought: But we speak the wisdom of God in a mystery, even the hidden wisdom, which God ordained before the world unto our glory: Which none of the princes of this world knew: for had they known it, they would not have crucified the Lord of glory.* Satan failed again as usual, he could not just help it because it is his nature to lose.

So whenever a bad situation or circumstance presents itself again, it is simply the loser presenting it. He has lost before presenting that situation and circumstance. See **John 16v33:** *I have told you these things, so that in Me you may have [perfect] peace and confidence. In the world you have tribulation and trials and distress and frustration; but be of good cheer [take courage; be confident, certain, undaunted]! For I have overcome the world. [I have deprived it of power to harm you and have conquered it for you.]* Do not be moved, it is what you prayed about and believed God for that will eventually manifest replacing the false situation or circumstance, amen.

The reason I win all the time is because I have God in me (you too) who is a winner all the time. I just can't help it, it's now my nature to win. No matter how it seems as if I will fail or be defeated; at the end of the day I come out a winner because that is my nature (the nature of God which I have put on.) **2 Corinthians 5v17:** *Therefore if any man be in Christ he is a new creature: old things are passed away; behold, all things are become new.*

Do you wonder why all things whether good or bad (that situation or circumstance) work for your good, because it has no choice. You have God in you who never fails, not defeated, conquers always in you. See **Romans 8v28:** *And we know that all things work together for good to them that love God, to them who are the called according to His purpose.*

By faith, you can only see the manifestation of who God is or what God says in the doing of His word. No matter how you pray or believe God for something, the evidence of those things you prayed about is only seen when you do the corresponding works to your faith. See **James 2v17:** *So also faith, if it does not have works (deeds and action of obedience to back it up), by itself is destitute of power (inoperative or dead).* The supernatural manifest itself or shows up during the process of doing the works aspect of faith. This is an important aspect of your faith or living by faith.

The word of God says, ask and you shall receive. From when you prayed asking, you immediately received as promised in the word (see **Matthew *7v7-8:* ** *ASK, and it shall be given you; seek, and ye shall find; knock and it shall be opened unto you: For every one that asketh receiveth; and he that seeketh findeth; and to him that knocketh it shall be opened.* Also **Daniel 10v12:** *Then said* he unto me, Fear not Daniel: for from the first day that thou didst set thine heart to understand, and to chasten thyself before thy God, thy words were heard, and I am come for thy words).The evidence that you actually received will be made manifest as you do the corresponding work of faith. So after praying and you sit down without carrying out any corresponding works, then you cannot see the result of your prayer prayed, because it is in the works it is made evident, that is the result. That is why we wonder why our prayer is not answered, the issue is not that it is not answered, the issue is you. You are not stepping out to do the works in order to see the evidence that your prayer was answered, **James 2vs 17, 20-22, 24 & 26:** *So also faith, if it does not have works (deeds and actions of obedience to back it up), by itself is destitute of power (inoperative, dead). Are you willing to be shown [proof], you foolish (unproductive, spiritually deficient) fellow that faith apart from [good] works is inactive and ineffective and worthless? Was not our forefather Abraham [shown to be] justified (made acceptable to God) by [his] works when he brought to the altar as an offering his [own] son Isaac.*

For as the body without the spirit is dead so faith without works is dead **James 2v26.**

For example, the bible says that "God is" **Hebrews 11v6:** *But without faith it is impossible to please Him: for he that cometh to God must believe that He is, and that He is a rewarder of them that deligently seek Him.* The fact that you pray to Him, attend church services and live right, is your corresponding works showing you believe that God is. If you are completely convinced about something, your words will prove it, your imagination, your deeds and action will all be in line with each other that you are convinced about that thing.

A man's faith is only seen by his works because faith is spiritual and cannot be seen physically but works can be seen. Doing corresponding works is actually taking or bringing your faith from the spiritual realm (unseen realm) to the physical realm where it can be seen; hence faith without corresponding works is dead.

Where does power lie, your words or God's?
Position yourself rightly, take sides with God.

3.

THE *WORD* OF GOD PART 1

There is absolute (tremendous) power in the word of God. It is life itself and Spirit, see **John 6v63b:** *the words that I speak unto you, they are spirit, and they are life.* The word is God Himself, **John 1v1:** *In the beginning was the Word, and the Word was with God, and the word was God.* It means your word is you, yourself.

God's word is not mere word. All things are upheld by the word of His power (**Hebrews 1v3:** *Who being the brightness of His glory, and the express image of His person, and upholding all things by the word of His power when He had by Himself purged our sins, sat down on the right hand of the Majesty on high*). The word of God is quick and powerful (**Hebrews 4v12**). No other power can stand God's power; and His strength lies in His word and His spirit. Therefore my strength lies in God's words, not my own words.

The measure of my strength is based on the amount of God's word I have in me, my believe in it, my meditation of it and my acting on it. Therefore my strength lies in the amount of God's word *imprinted* in my spirit.

You must always be in agreement with the word of God, (your opinion does not matter); having oneness of mind with God through His word, **Amos 3v3**: *Can two walk together, except they be agreed?* My thoughts, deeds and actions are further confirmation or proof that I am in agreement with God's word. Remember when two or three agree concerning something it shall be done. You and God in agreement, then it is settled, it is a done deal, amen.

You cannot experience God outside His word. Any word spoken outside of God's word is not truth. Only God's word is truth. God will back up every of His word you speak but He will not back up any other word that is not His word.

Any word spoken outside of God's word is devoid of power and does not have God's backing. Satan knows this and therefore thrives on words spoken outside God's words to accuse you before God even if he had influenced you in speaking that unbelief.

God's word is final authority. It is also the highest form of reality.

What is the root of unbelief? And how do we tackle it? Find out how to kill unbelief because it is the obstacle between you and the fulfilment of your dream and seeing the manifestation of the things you prayed about. Unbelief, a tool the devil has used to steal a lot from us.

3.

UNBELIEF

Unbelief is challenging the ability of God and doubting His integrity. How? By our words, actions and motives when they are in contrary to His word.

Unbelief stems from responding or reacting to circumstances and situations rather than staying focused on His word or that we have requested for in prayer.

When a circumstance or situation is not in line with what we prayed about or for, unbelief starts to rise up. As pressure is added by Satan to that circumstance or situation, the unbelief continues to grow until it reaches the point where it now completely replaces the initial belief we had in our hearts whether for something or somebody. The devil's intention is plain, he knows that God does not honour or respond to unbelief therefore the pressure; hence you deny yourself of that thing which you have asked God for because of unbelief and Satan has stolen from you.

Sources of unbelief are usually from your physical senses (hearing, seeing, feeling etc) and from your mind (thoughts, imaginations, etc).

Remember what you hear, see and feel changes. Your thoughts and imaginations are dynamic, hence unstable. The devil therefore uses them to play tricks on our minds. But when your mind is saturated by the unchanging word of God, you cannot be tricked because the devil cannot toss God's word to and fro, there is no loophole in God's word (like your own thoughts) and hence Satan cannot penetrate it.

God refers to the unbelieving heart as an evil heart. **Unbelief is saying God is not able**. As Christians, we are careful not to verbally say this but our words, actions speak it loud and clear. Others claim in deniance that 'we are not saying God is not able but that they prefer to do things by themselves'. This is obviously trusting in themselves more than God. At some point we have been guilty of this.

So how do we deal with this issue of unbelief?

Solutions to unbelief;

1. **Studying the word of God.** See **Hosea 4v6a:** *My people are destroyed for lack of knowledge* and **2 Timothy 2v15:** *Study to show thyself approved unto God, a work-*

man that needed not to be ashamed, rightly dividing the word of truth.*

2. **Taking the word of God from the bible and putting it in our hearts by MEDITATION.** See **Joshua 1v8** : *This book of the law shall not depart out of thy mouth; but thou shall meditate therein day and night, that thou mayest observe to do according to all that is written therein: for then thou shalt make thy way prosperous, and then thou shalt have good success.* Remember *for the letter killeth but the spirit giveth life* (**2 Corinthians 3v6b**).

3. **Confessing it.** Speak it loud for your ears to hear. See **Joshua 1v8:** *This book of the law shall not depart out of thy mouth….* And **Romans 10v10b:**….*and with the mouth confession is made unto salvation.*

4. **Trusting the integrity of the word of God for it is impossible for God to lie.** **Hebrews *6v17-18*:** *Wherein God willing more abundantly to shew unto the heirs of promise the immutability of His counsel, confirmed it by an oath: That by two immutable things, in which it was impossible for God to lie, we might have a strong consolation, who have fled for refuge to lay hold upon the hope set before us.*

The more we trust God by believing His word and taking Him for His word, the less our unbelief.

Why do we not see and receive the maximum blessings in our lives despite working so hard on our jobs and some of us giving tithe and offering regularly? This chapter is an eye opener for progress in our finances which will in turn enable us to partake more in the vision of expanding our father's kingdom on earth.

4.

MONEY

What you expose yourself to determines your level of blessing or extent of what you get out of it. The more you expose yourself to something, the more you get out of that thing or the more you move higher or progress up the ladder. For example the more you expose yourself to God, being more committed, loving God more, the more evidence of God and His abundance you will see in your life. You will also be more Christ like as a result of giving more of yourself to Him.

The quantity of water in a stream and that in the ocean are different with the ocean having more water as we are aware. Note, God will only give you the blessing of a stream if that is what you avail yourself to, because you determine the level or extent of your blessing by what you avail yourself to. See **2 kings 4v1-6:** *Now there cried a certain woman of the wives of the sons of the prophets unto Elisha, saying, Thy servant my husband is dead; and thou knowest that thy servant did fear the LORD: and the creditor is come to take unto him my two sons to be bondmen. And Elisha said unto her, what shall I do for thee ? Tell me, what hast thou in the house? And she said, Thine handmaid hath not any thing in the house, save a pot of oil.* **Then he said, Go, borrow thee vessels abroad of all thy neighbours, even empty vessels; borrow not a few.** *And when thou art come in, thou shalt shut the door upon thee and upon thy sons, and shalt pour out into all those vessels, and thou shall set aside that which is full. So she went from him, and shut the door upon her and upon her sons, who brought the vessels to her; and she poured out. And it came to pass, when the vessels were full, that she said unto her son, Bring me yet a vessel. And he said unto her, There is not a vessel more. And the oil stayed.* The widow was not restricted to a specify number of vessels she should get so she determined the level of her blessing by the quantity of the vessels she got. If she got more vessels she should have had more blessings.

The blessing of God cannot be measured or quantified, you determine how much of it you want.

So God will give the blessing of an ocean to another (more abundance) because this person availed himself to greater prospects. So if it's a blessing of water, the person exposed to the ocean will get more than the one exposed to a stream. This is not because God is partial, no. It is because you have to avail yourself to a physical environment (fertile place), to where there is no physical limitations to what you get. So when our God of seasons and of the harvest visits you, your rain of blessings is overflowing because you positioned yourself where there is no physical restrictions to your blessing; so you experience the full measure of God's abundance.

When you work 9am-5pm, which is the usual time many people do their regular job, there is already a fixed annual salary placed on you. If your salary is between for example £10,000 and £20,000, when God promotes you in that job, the maximum blessing you can receive is £20,000 only because that is capped or fixed maximum amount to be paid for that job. You cannot compare yourself to someone else who has no restrictions on what he can receive. This brings me to an example of the stock market, no salaries to be received (if you are an independent trader), no limitations on what you can receive; so don't expect the man doing 9-5pm to get the same degree of financial blessing when the God of harvest visits both him and the stock market trader, no. The stock market trader will definitely get more because there are no physical rules, laws or limitations placed on what he can receive so he has an opportunity to manifest more of the abundance of God's blessings financially in his life because he has positioned himself rightly.

For the man who works 9am-5pm, he must take out his salary and place it into something where there is no restrictions on how much he is allowed to take out as profit (e.g stock market), otherwise the maximum of God's blessings is not made manifest in him as it should because he has not positioned himself rightly.

Also the man that owns his own business is likely to experience God's abundance more than the man that works 9am-5pm because he does not have a fixed income on himself so when the God of harvest visits him, abundance is made manifest.

Remember God does not restrict or aportion this quantity or amount of blessing to this person and another amount to another. God is the God of super abundance; you (man) placed a limitation on your own blessing by where you positioned yourself, so God is not partial.

Always be in direct contact with your money or business so that God does not have to pass through a third party to get your blessing to you. Experience God's blessings first hand by working for yourself. Your tithe and offering will increase because you will definitely experience the first hand blessing of God.

The man that lets his money work for him and the one that works for his money are different. The first one gets more reward and the second less. You are either in the first category or the second category but some people go on to do both, taking the money they work for and converting it to the money that works for him because that is where the great reward is. Until you get out of the second category of people which is what most people do (the masses), the full measure of your prosperity cannot be experienced.

The reason why many of us Christians do not see or experience the measure of abundance of what we will like is because we only work for money and not allowing money to work for us, hence not experiencing the full measure of our blessing. We as Christians must think how money can work for us. Pray about God's leading; read magazines, financial newspapers, newspapers about businesses and people's ideas. Acquire knowledge, then set your mind thinking like it has never thought and the Holy Spirit in all of this as you search and think, will lead you to what you should be doing. Act on the instructions or leadings of the Holy Spirit no matter how small it is; watch your seed grow, that idea or suggestion.

Prayer, a demonstration of our faith. What are also the benefits of it?

6.

PRAYER

Prayer is communication and fellowship with our father. It is a demonstration of our total reliance on God and not on ourselves. The bible says in **1Samuel 2v9b:** *for by strength shall no man prevail.*

When you pray, it is an evidence that you believe God is and that He exist, because you will not speak to someone you think does not exist.

God almighty delights in our prayer, see **Proverbs 15v8:** *The sacrifice of the wicked is an abomination to the LORD: but the prayer of the upright is His delight.*

When I pray, I am demonstrating the fact that He has a place in my life not verbally only but in my action (which is prayer). I am telling God I cannot do it myself but that I need Him.

Prayer builds your faith.

My faith level increases when I pray (actually during my prayer time my confidence and my trust in God increases) but after prayer, I feel the 'high' for some hours and then it fizzles. It is important to maintain that faith at that level attained during prayer and one way of doing this is to remember you are still in the presence of God after you leave your prayer place or room. The truth is that we never realy leave His presence but as men we tend to forget. We are continually (24 hours) in the divine presence of God, and not when we are literally praying, see **Matthew 28v20b;** *and behold, I am with you all the days (perpetually, uniformly, and on every occasion), to the [very] close and comsummation of the days* and **Ephesians 2v6:** *And hath raised us up together, and made us sit together in heavenly places in Christ Jesus.*

Prayer uplifts your mind.

Personally I may be feeling down before praying but after praying I feel uplifted, praise God. **Psalm 16v11 says:** *....in God's presence is fulness of joy.*

Prayer helps you to make the right decision despite your feelings.

I may want to make a decision which is not in line with God's word because of a prevailing circumstance (for example anger, hurt) and I am so full of it, but going into the presence of God in prayer even if it is the last thing I want to do and I am not in the mood, even if it is like a routine, my decision definitely change and align itself with God's word.

Prayer helps you to forgive, hence you are restored.

Forgiveness for that person that offended or hurt me becomes easier because when I pray I release that person that hurt me and I feel the peace of God again.

Prayer restores hope.

No matter how hopeless my situation may look and sometimes I have almost given up or I have even given up; my hope is restored again when I tell it to the father in prayer.

Prayer gives God a go ahead to act on your behalf.

The bible says in **Psalms 91v15:** *He shall call upon me, and I will answer him: I will be with him in trouble; I will deliver him, and honour him.*

There are other benefits of prayer not mentioned here. But it's importance and necessity is obvious as seen in the life of our Lord Jesus Christ who always prayed. Let us therefore follow in His footsteps until it becomes part of us.

Meditation, an entrance to our spirit man. Unveil your innerman and receive answers to your problems then watch your progress.

7.

MEDITATION

For those that do not understand what meditation is; it is actually taking the word of God, any scripture (for example, taking the word of God that says with God all things are possible) and you think about it, ponder it, ruminate on it. And it could be you are trying to know the meaning, and before you know it the Holy Spirit shows up taking you by the hand 'around town' that is enlightening your understanding, (taking your mind to different examples that you will by yourself not think about) and at the end of the session with the Holy Spirit, you have known more and you have a deeper and clearer understanding of that word of God.

You find the Holy Spirit in your place of meditation. You definitely find Him anytime you meditate on the word of God and He always teaches you during these periods. Meditation somehow brings you into your spirit man (inner man) which is the real you recreated after the image and likeness of God.

For example, you walk through a particular road and you always meet this person on this road each time you pass there; so is meditation, you always meet the Holy Spirit but this time this person you meet interacts with you, teaches you, exposes so many things to you within such a short time, you will know you have met Him. Remember, anytime you feel He is no longer there, go to where you can find Him and that is meditation.

I am beginning to think that meditation has a link with the spiritual realm since you meet the Holy Spirit there.

Does it mean we should always go to where we find the Holy Spirit? Of course yes. As Christians, it means we should continually meditate on the word of God and the Holy Spirit will always show up and always teach us. No wonder God said what He said in **Joshua 1v8:** *This book of the law shall not depart out of thy mouth; but thou shalt meditate therein day and night, that thou mayest observe to do according to all that is written therein: for then thou shalt make thy way prosperous, and then thou shall have good success.*

When what you received during meditation is put into practice or exercised, it transforms your life completely. The truth is that at the end of the meditation session with the Holy Spirit, you immediately feel your life has been changed already by what He has taught you. But when you leave there and you forget about it, then you are not able to exercise it and before you know it, it fades into the background without you then profiting maximally from it.

Every session with the Holy Spirit must be guarded, valued and treasured. What He has taught us must be exercised in our lives on a continual basis in order for us to always see the result of what we have been taught.

The essence of meditation is for the word of God to take roots in our hearts, enabling us to have a heart knowledge of it rather than head knowledge. By this, it is then easier to put it into practice. See **2 Corinthians 3v6:** *Who also hath made us able ministers of the new testament; not of the letter, but of the spirit: for the letter killeth, but the spirit giveth life.*

Note, periods of meditation are also where we can find solutions to our problems. As we meditate on a scipture, the Holy Spirit will somehow lead us to the solution we needed for the problem.

Meditation also helps us in making the right decisions that can change our lives because you meet with the Spirit of Truth who directs us.

Remember the Holy Spirit will guide us into all truth, **John16v13:** *Howbeit when he, the Spirit of truth, is come, he will guide you into all truth: for he shall not speak of himself; but whatsoever he shall hear, that shall he speak: and he will shew you things to come.*

Who do we trust? Ourselves or God? Why should we trust God, find out yourself as you read.

8.

TRUSTING IN GOD

Trusting in God guarantees entering His rest. You cannot talk about entering God's rest without talking about trusting God. What does entering God's rest entail;

(A) Absolute trust in God
(B) Dependence on the leading of the Holy Spirit

Remember the word of God that said, *'those that trust in the Lord shall be as mount Zion, which cannot be removed, but abideth forever'* **Psalm 125v1.**

The more you know God, the easier it becomes for you to let go of anxiety and worry and trust Him. You do not trust someone you do not know. The extent to which you know God will determine the level of trust you have for Him.

How do you know God? By studying His word and meditating on it. You cannot know God outside His word,

See **John 1v1**: *IN the beginning was the Word, and the Word was God, and the Word was God*. If you do not know God, then you cannot say you trust Him.

Absolute trust in God brings about perfect peace in your life. Remember the word in **Isaiah 26v3** that says '*You will guard him and keep him in perfect and constant peace whose mind [both its inclination and its character] is stayed on You, because he commits himself to You, leans on You, and hopes confidently in you*'. He will keep in perfect peace that whose mind is stayed on Him'.

Trusting God also entails total (complete) surrender of every aspect of your life for Him to guide you through the Holy Spirit.

Reasons why you should trust God

God always has your good in mind.

'*For I know the thoughts that I think towards you, saith the LORD, thoughts of peace, and not of evil, to give you an expected end*' **Jeremiah 29v11**.

God loves you

'*He spared not His only son from you, but delivered Him up for us all, how shall He not with Him also freely give us all things*' **Romans 8v32**.

His love is immense and unconditional. Even when we were yet sinners, Christ died for us. See **Romans 5v8**: *But God commended his love towards us, in that, while we were yet sinners, Christ died for us.*

God's word is infallible

His word does not pass away but abideth forever. No word of His return to Him void. He watches over every of His word to perform it. See **Matthew 24v35:** *Heaven and earth shall pass away, but my words shall not pass away* and **Isaiah 55v11:** *So shall My word be that goes forth out of My mouth: it shall not return to me void [without producing any effect, useless] but it shall accomplish that which I please and purpose, and it shall prosper in the thing for which I sent it.* Also **Jeremiah 29v12:** *Then said the Lord to me, You have seen well, for I am alert and active, watching over My word to perform it.*

God is our helper.

He is our present help all the time. He said *'He shall call upon Me, and I will answer him; I will be with him in trouble, I will deliver him and honour him'* **Psalm 91v15.** Convince yourself God is always there for you because He is. *'For I the LORD thy God will hold thy right hand, saying unto thee, Fear not; I will help thee'* **Isaiah 41v13.**

God's grace is available to us.

It is always available. This unmerited favour grants us access to the throne of God. **Hebrews 4v16:** *Let us therefore come boldly unto the throne of grace, that we may obtain help in time of need.* Also see **Ephesians 2v8:** *For by grace are ye saved through faith; and that not of yourselves: it is the gift of God.*

God is a covenant keeper.

Covenant makes one obliged. God is obliged to you through His covenant, see **Psalm 111v5b:** *He will ever be mindful of His convenant.* God does not and will not break covenant. We have an everlasting covenant with Him. **Acts 3v25:** *Ye are the children of the prophets, and of the covenant which God made with our fathers, saying unto Abraham, And in thy seed shall all the kindreds of the earth be blessed.*

We are heirs of God and Co-heirs with Christ.

Recognise that this is who you are, a child of God ; **Romans 8v17:** *And if children, then heirs; heirs of God, and joint-heirs with Christ; if so be that we suffer with him, that we may be also glorified together.* You therefore have an inheritance through Christ (Abraham's seed).

God is your father.

'*Our Father which art in heaven*' **Luke 11v2a**. Also '*we were born (again) not of blood nor of the will of the flesh nor of the will of man but of God*; hence God is our father, **John 1v13**.

You cannot trust someone you have no relationship with. The level you trust is dependent on your level of relationship with that person.

If you who are evil knows to give good gifts to your children, how much more shall my father in heaven give good gift to us that ask Him, knowing we are His children.

Remember trusting God comes from knowing Him personally.

He stands at the door of your heart knocking and ready to come in and dine with you if you let Him in, amen.

Your mind or the word of God, where does your victory lie?
Find out yourself and remove the limitations from your life.

9.

THE WORD OF GOD   PART 2

Whenever you operate from your mind, you are operating from a zone of limitations but whenever you operate from the word of God, you are operating from the zone of no limitations.

You limit yourself whenever you act from your mind. No matter how good you are in using your mind in reasonings and using it logically you will come face to face with limitations.

God not only gave us His word, but went further to guarantee the fact that it works, **Isaiah 55v11;** *So shall My word be that goes forth out of My mouth: it shall not return to me void [without producing any effect, useless] but it shall accomplish that which I please and purpose, and it shall prosper in the thing for which I sent it.* **Hebrews 6v16-19:** *For men verily swear by the greater: and an oath for confirmation is to them an end of all strife. Wherein God,* *willing more abundantly to shew unto the heirs of promise the immutability of his counsel, confirmed it by an oath: That by two immutable things, in which it was impossible for God to lie, we might have a strong consolation, who have fled for refuge to lay hold upon the hope set before us: which hope we have as an anchor of the soul, both sure and steadfast, and which entereth into that within the veil;*

God's word is Himself (**John 1v1:** *IN the beginning was the Word, and the Word was with God, and the Word was God*) and if God fails in His word, that means God has failed Himself and it is absolutely impossible for God to fail Himself; this further proves the authenticity of His word. So God will ensure His word always come to pass because His word is Himself.

So as a child of God, you need to convince yourself of the word of God and that it works, believe it, then change your thinking to conform to that word He has spoken about you or to you (from the bible) just like Abraham did. Abraham no longer saw his body dead or Sarah's womb dead despite her age; that means Abraham changed his thinking to be in alignment, to conform to what God had promised him (that is God's word given to him just like the word of God from the bible to us) and he got his miracle. See **Romans 4v19-20:** *And being not weak in faith, he considered not his own body now dead, when he was about an hundred years old, neither yet the deadness of Sarah's womb; he staggered not at the promise of God through unbelief; but was strong in faith, giving glory to God.*

Always convince yourself of God's word first, then change your thinking into His thoughts which is His word.

I also wish to mention here that what man calls impossibilities are actually things that are either beyond his knowledge or not yet discovered, so man regards these as impossibilities. The truth is that though these things have not been discovered by man or are beyond man's knowledge does not make them impossibilities, these are limitations of a man. But beyond these all is a zone where things which appear like limitation (that is, the impossibilities of a man) are actually possibilities and that is the word of God. The word of God is the light that gives light to everything yet to be discovered or beyond man's knowledge, **Proverbs 8v12:** *I wisdom dwell with prudence, and find out knowledge of witty inventions.* The word of God is a zone of no limitations.

Remember the blind cannot lead the blind; man cannot tell you this or that are impossibilities or limitations in your life; why ? because they are men and only see and know that much. Step into the zone where the sighted sees the way (which is the word of God)and leads all the blind men. See **Psalm 119v105:** *Thy word is a lamp unto my feet, and a light unto my path.*

You have **NO LIMITATIONS** in the **WORD** of **GOD** and it is the zone of unlimited successes where God wants us to always operate from.

Remember after convincing yourself of God's word and you have changed your thoughts to conform to His, do not ask questions like how will this be? Do not search or try to find out how God will do it because in using your logical reasonings, unbelief steps in and nullify your faith. Unbelief comes as a result of you coming face to face with your limitation which is reasoning from your mind. Stop being logical because whenever you try to operate from your mind, you will always meet limitation and all sorts of negative thoughts set in. Leave that zone and come into light (no limitation) which is the word of God. This is faith itself.

Our dreams and goals are seeds of our future. How do we realise them?

10.

THE INVISIBLE THAT BECOMES THE VISIBLE

Your dream is your invisible companion accompanying you from your present into your future according to a great man of God.

If you cannot see the future (imagine it, "picturise" it), you cannot get there. Let your heart grasp your destination. Call things that be not (things you see in the future, your imagination, picture, dream) as if they are now. By doing this, you are actually bringing your dream, your future into the now.

God does not deal with your dream (which is a seed) as if it is in the future but in the now; that is why He calls things that be not (for a man, they are not because they are not yet seen, but to God they are now) as though they were, **Romans 4v17b:** …..*even God, who quickened the dead, and calleth those things that be not as though they were.*

God is a Spirit, He recognises your dream as viable (like an unborn baby in the womb). It is real and tangible and God deals with it that way. It does not become visible first before God treats it as visible. Man does the opposite, because man is physical. This explains why you can sin at the thought level (for example thinking about fornication)without actually physically committing the act because it is real to God in the invisible realm. God deals with the invisible and remember that your seed or dream or vision are in the same realm He operates which is the invisible realm.

By speaking consistently and repeatedly the word of God that is linked to your dream (that is calling things that be not as though they were), your dream becomes more and more real to you.

What you see in your mind you eventually become or achieve or have.

You have to link your present to your future (example like a bridge) in order to get to the future. God linked the present to the future when He changed ABRAM's name to ABRAHAM (father of many nations). God used the present as a seed, ABRAM (the NAME) to link the future ABRAHAM. God took something of the present to link the future. See **Genesis 17v4-5:** *As for me, behold, my covenant is with thee, and thou shalt be a father of many nations. Neither shall thy name any more be called Abram, but thy name shall be Abraham; for a father of many nations have I made thee.*

What you do today will determine what your tomorrow will be. Look at your yesterday it is linked to your today. Therefore know that your today will be linked to your tomorrow.

Debts, loans or credit cards is formed from the idea of bringing (which is actually stealing) from your tomorrow into your today. In essence going into your future indirectly to steal from it. Avoid anything that goes into your tomorrow which is your future; to steal, kill and destroy.

The devil came to steal, to kill and to destroy not just your today but your tomorrow. But satan cannot personally go into your future, so he steals your tomorrow from your today by something he causes you to do, say, today; knowing that your tomorrow is linked to your today. If satan steals your tomorrow from your today, the consequences does not immediately manifest today until your tomorrow.

Your everyday imput to your seed is your season of preparation. The seed goes through all the processes until it germinates. There is always a period between sowing and reaping, causes and consequences. Sowing is what you do today or say etc. Reaping is what you get tomorrow. So what you get tomorrow is determined by what you do today. Sowing links your today to your tomorrow.

You become what you consistently think about, for as a man thinketh so he is. See **Proverbs 23v7a:** *For as he thinks in his heart, so he is.* Your thinking and meditating is sowing, continue in it and it will manifest. Sowing (the present) and reaping (your future) is linking your today to your tomorrow and your present to your future. Remember plant or sow the right seed to reap the right harvest.

Remember the dream in you is viable (it is a seed) and is alive today in the now not in the future because the future is simply the manifestation of what has been, (which is the seed); the invisible becoming the visible.

Having difficulties in your marriage? This is a MUST chapter to demonstrate the overcomer you are and for the marriage to continue till death do you part.

11.

DIVORCE ("THORN IN THE FLESH")

The true reason behind divorce goes beyond the physical. It is not " INCOMPATIBILITY " as the world has defined it as the cause of many divorces. Divorce happens as a result of a person not facing up to their spouse's atitude or character and changing his own behaviour (not the spouse), in order for peace to prevail in the marriage regardless of the spouse's atitude or character or that prevailing bad circumstance or situation.

Do not look at the other person that is your spouse to change but you have to change in order to overcome that bad prevalent circumstance or situation. You have to learn to live above that circumstance, so you can have a joyful, peaceful and happy marriage regardless of the situation and circumstance.

So you may ask, how do you deal with this circumstance and overcome especially when you think you are right. Also despite praying that God should change your spouse, he seem to have hardly changed, then what do you do? See Paul in **2 Corinthians 12 v7-9a:** *And lest I should be exalted above measure through the abundance of the revelations, there was given to me a thorn in the flesh, the messenger of Satan to buffet me, lest I should be exalted above measure. For this thing I besought the Lord thrice, that it may depart from me. And he said unto me, My grace is sufficient for thee: for my strength is made perfect in weakness.* He prayed three times to God to remove the thorn in his flesh that satan put on him (the devil not being aware it was serving a useful purpose). God did not remove the thorn but instead told Paul "My grace is sufficient for you, for my (God) strength is made perfect in weakness". Then your first approach is to remember God's grace is sufficient for you and that the "thorn" which is the problem or repeatative problem shaking the marriage God might not always remove instantly.

What does it mean to be an "overcomer"? It is succeeding from the inside to the outside (not vice versa), prevailing over the presenting circumstance and situation. The devil always operate most times through circumstances and situations but God from the inside of a man. Since you do not have control over the prevailing circumstance and situation, then you have to deal with it from where your strength lies which is the inner man. Let the word of God rise from inside of you, you take it and do it by acting on it and by doing this you are able to demonstrate the overcomer the word says you are.

You cannot show you are an overcomer without overcoming something. For example being able to live with your spouse despite who he is, by you changing your atitude and character to conform to God's word for peace to prevail even if you think you are right and your spouse is wrong. Now what is the fruit of the spirit? See **Galatians 5v22-23:** *they are LOVE, JOY, PEACE, LONGSUFFERING, GENTLENESS, GOODNESS, FAITH, MEEKNESS, TEMPERANCE, against such there is no law.* These are in the bible for us 'to do'. What about **Proverbs 10v12:** *Hatred stirreth up strifes: but love covereth all sins.* Have you come to a point where your love covers all the sins of your spouse, his atitude, character etc.

You see if you think divorce is the way out in your marriage, you are mistaken. The atitude or character in your spouse you could not overcome or deal with while in marriage you will later face again in life. It is still a challenge awaiting you in the future and when it surfaces again because it will; there will be no way out then. With divorce, you tell yourself you have completely eliminated the problem but unfortunately you did not. Because it is about you dealing with a situation or circumstance from the inside of you, you arising and prevailing over it rather than divorcing as a way of eliminating that circumstance or situation in a physical way. The devil sees your weaknesses and will always make sure you have many of such similar circumstances and situations come your way so you can fall into them in order to steal other things from you. Remember the bible said satan came to steal, kill and destroy, **John 10v10a:** *The thief cometh not, but for to steal, and to kill, and to destroy.*

Sometimes divorce is just a sign of an already existing type of atitude or character or pattern of doing things in a person. For example take someone who has always dealt with his problem by blaming every other person, circumstance and situation except himself. Since he has never seen in himself that he may have a fault; and he ever experiences divorce anytime in life, he is only manifesting that character or atitude of his life he had not dealt with.

Divorce is normally requested by the less tolerant party (spouse) who is trying to change or deal with the circumstance or situation without actually changing his own atitude or character and overcoming the presenting situation or circumstance in order for the marriage to work.

Know that when the devil knows you are no longer responding negatively to that circumstance and situation and you continuing that way, then the devil will flee as the bible said resist the devil and he will flee. See **James 4v7:** *Submit yourselves therefore to God. Resist the devil, and he will flee from you.*

As a christian, married, most times we will not have many of our trials and temptations out of the house, the most trials you will get will be within your home. So how do you build yourself as a christian? Capitalise on the circumstance and situation in your marriage which is your spouse's atitude or offensive character to you to build up the image of Christ in yourself. See Paul again in **2 Corinthians 12 v7-9**, he did not quit preaching or excelling in the things of God because of the 'thorn in his flesh'; Paul excelled regardless or despite of it; so you can too and God's strength showed strong on his behalf. So remain in your marriage despite or regardless of the circumstance. I remember the saying "quitters never win" and "winners never quit". Winners face up to a situation or circumstance, deals with it from the inside out while quitters do not face up to themselves as the problem solvers but rather deal with the circumstance and situation to try to eliminate the problem and when this does not change, they quit or if their spouse do not change, they quit by divorcing.

Remember the very 'thorn in your marriage' being used by the devil in order to try to dissolve your marriage, is what will bring out the overcomer in you and turn your thorn into a blessing. Make a good purpose out of the 'thorn' intended to destroy you, for that thorn have a useful purpose in disguise.

God bless every couple that will read this because the Holy Spirit through what you have read, will bring healing to the worst of marriages even healing and unity again to those who have already submitted their divorce papers and unite those already divorced in Jesus name, amen.

Remember God will always heal marriages, He designed this excellent institution; let Him. See **Genesis 2vs18,22-24:** *AND the LORD God said, It is not good that the man should be alone; I will make him an help meet for him. And the rib, which the LORD God had taken from man, made he a woman, and brought her unto the man. And Adam said, This is now bone of my bones, and flesh of my flesh: she shall be called Woman, because she was taken out of Man. Therefore shall a man leave his father and his mother, and shall cleave unto his wife: and they shall be one flesh.*

If you are reading this book and you are not born again, you can get saved now and instantly become a child of God as you say the prayer below;

PRAYER OF SALVATION

Lord, I come to you the way I am, a sinner. I cannot change myself except you change me. I recognise that Jesus Christ came into the world to save me and not to condemn me. I acknowledge that He died for me. Today therefore in agreement with your word, I confess with my mouth the Lord Jesus and believe in my heart that God raised Him from the dead. I receive Him right now as my Lord. Thank you Lord for saving me in Jesus name, amen.

If you have just said this prayer for the first time, you are now a born again child of God. I encourage you to look for an evangelical or pentecostal church in your area to start attending in order for you to learn more so you can grow and mature as a christian.

God bless you.

We are happy to hear from you about how this book has been a blessing to you. Send your testimony to this email address; lifeasrevealed@yahoo.com

In need of a motivational Speaker for your church group, conference or meetings or to give a talk on any of the topics covered within this book; contact me at this email address; lifeasrevealed@yahoo.com.

Printed in the United States
62482LVS00002B/1-348